Mike Disfarmer

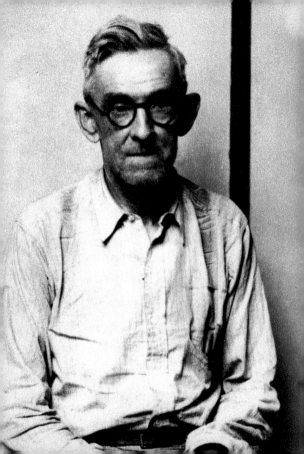

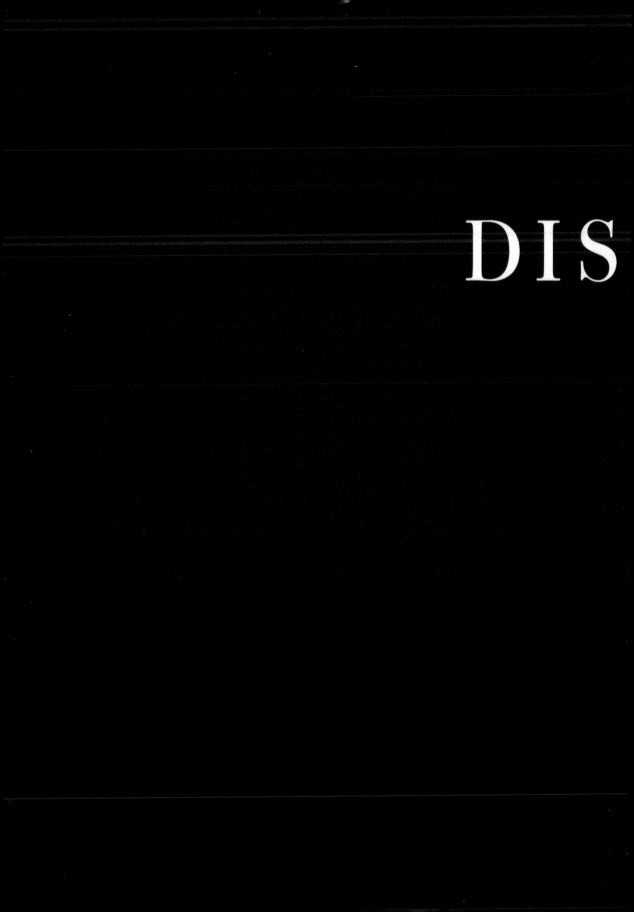

DIS

1939–1946

Heber Springs Portraits

FARMER

From the Collections of

Peter Miller and Julia Scully

Essay by Julia Scully

Twin Palms Publishers 1996

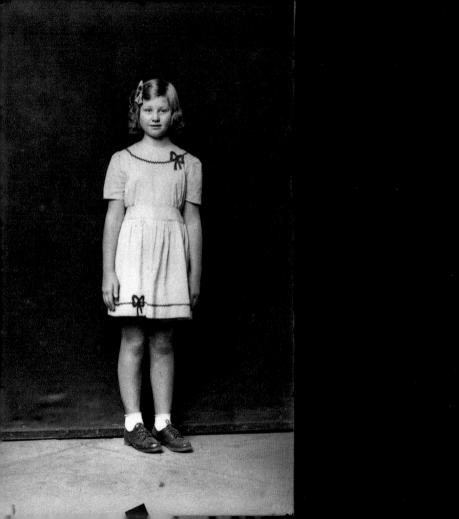

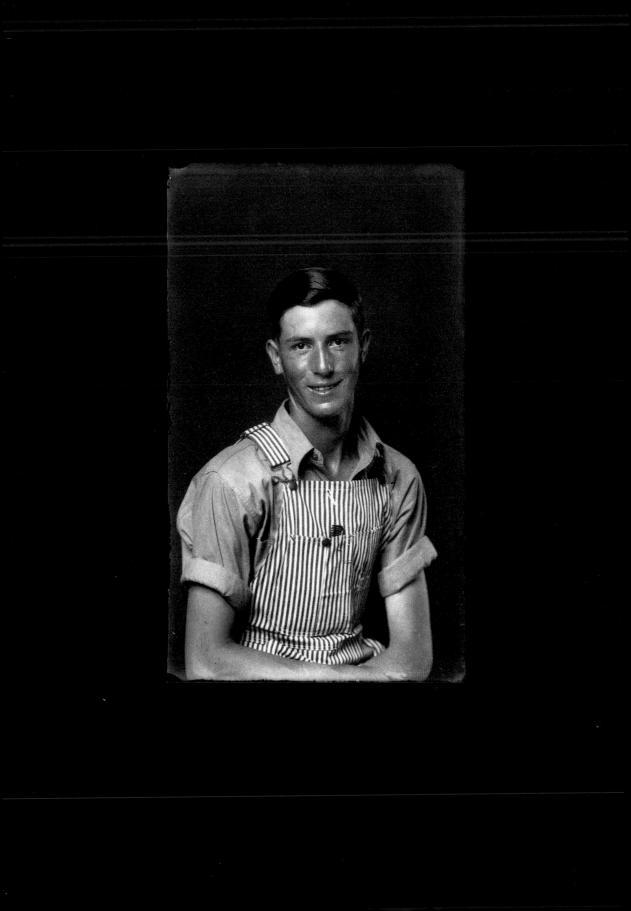

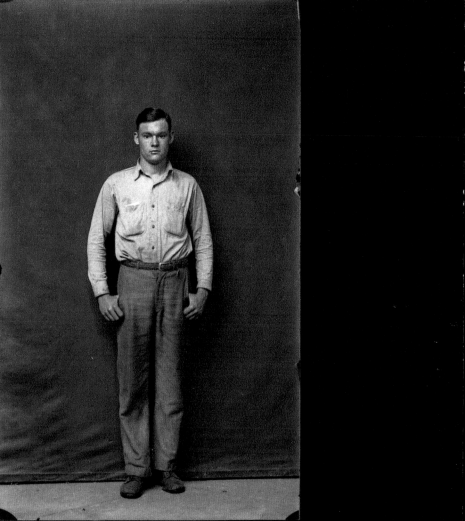

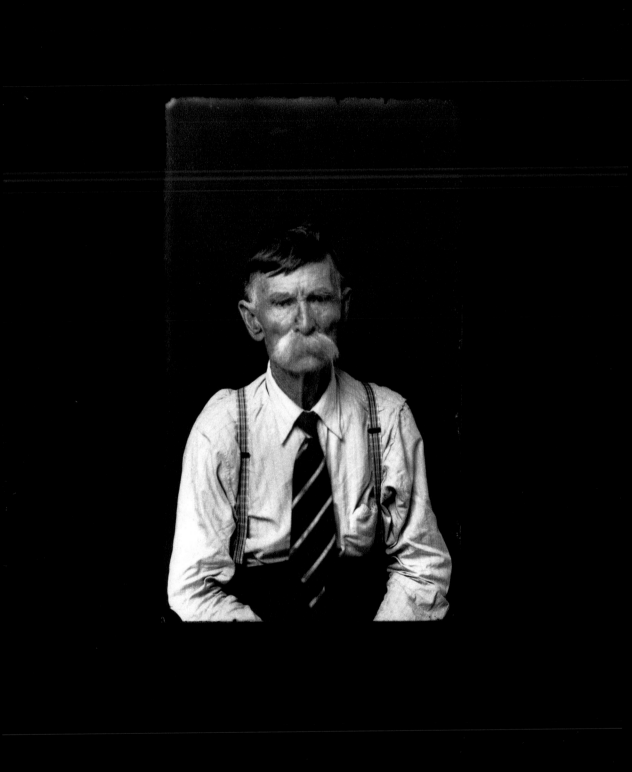

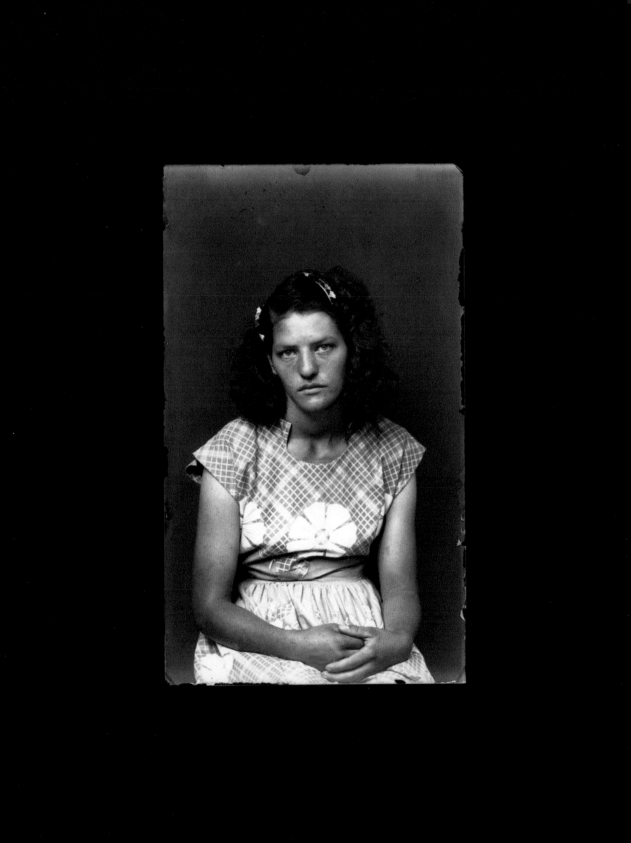

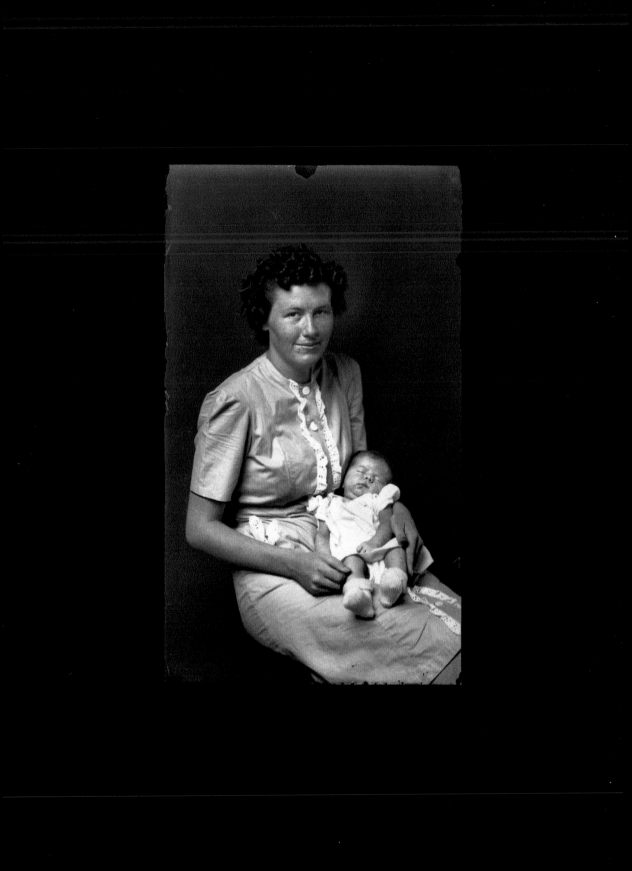

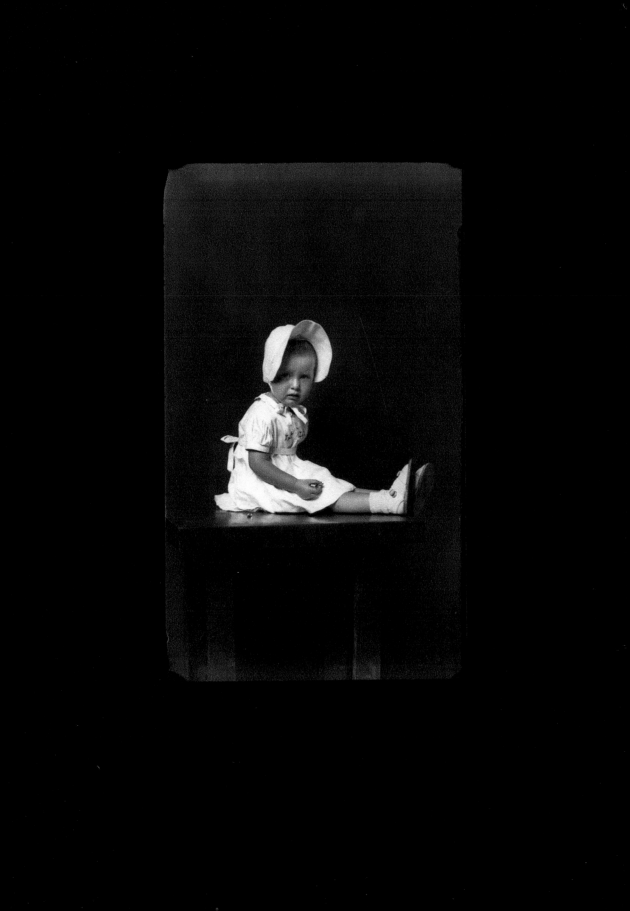

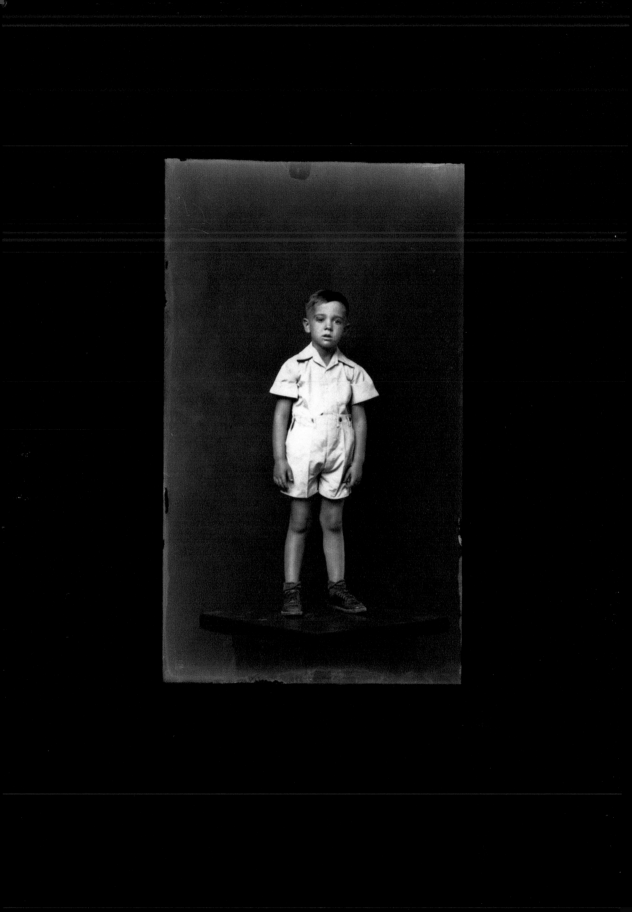

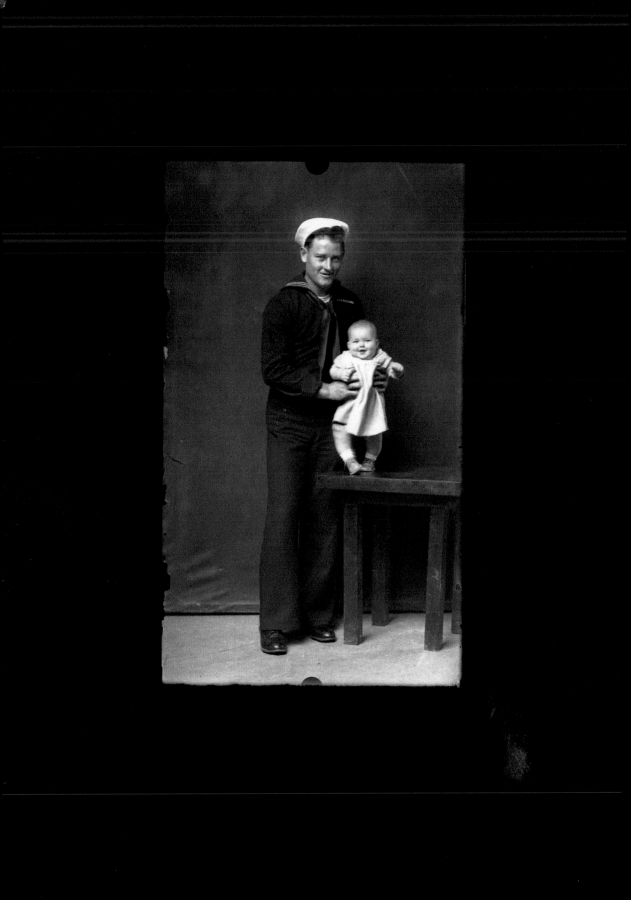

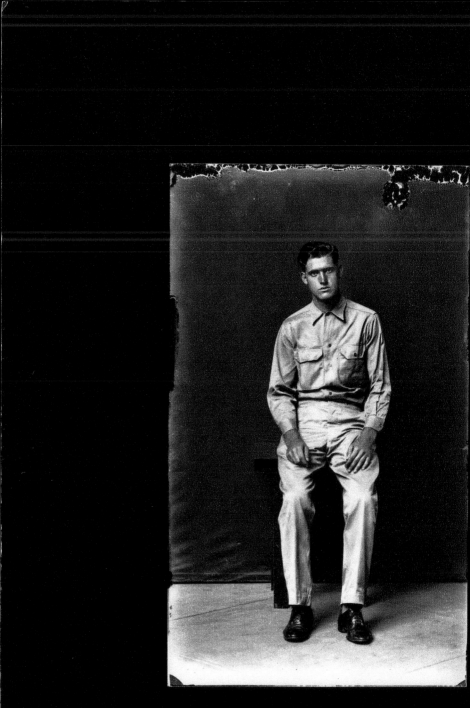

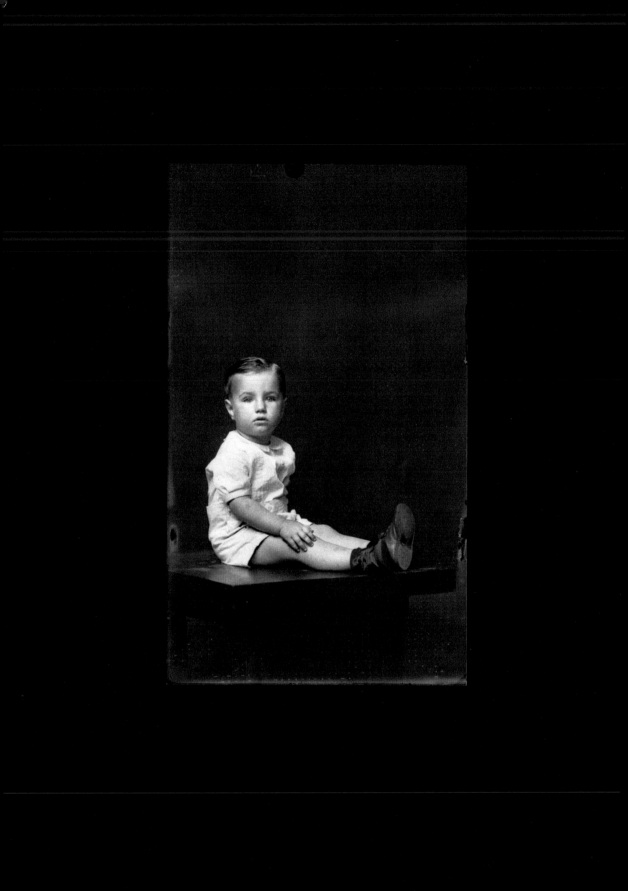

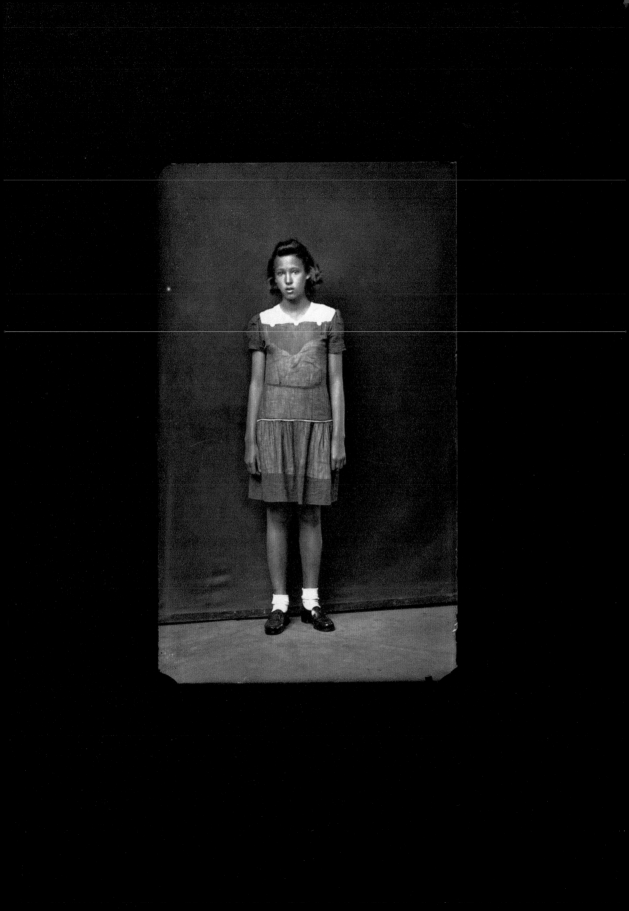

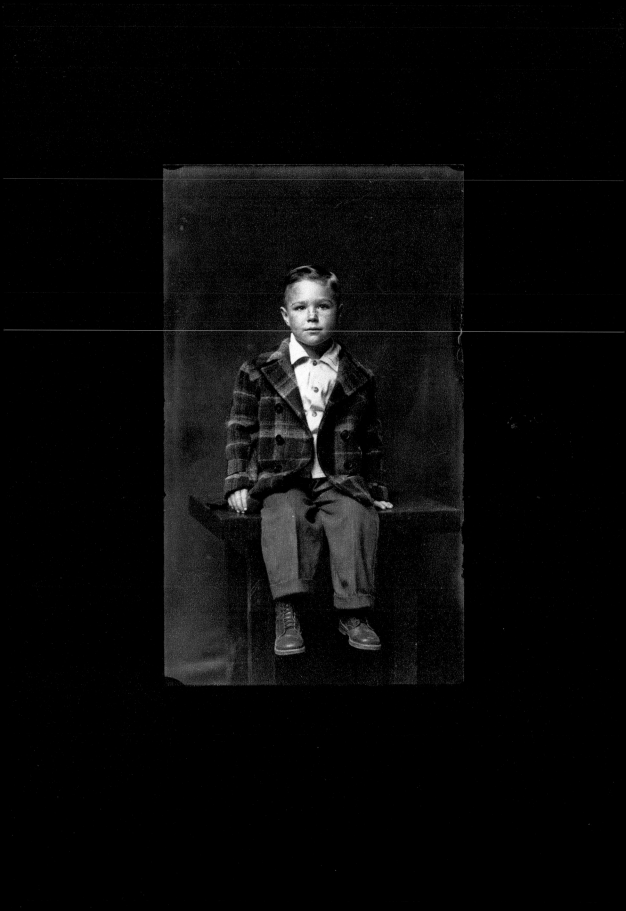

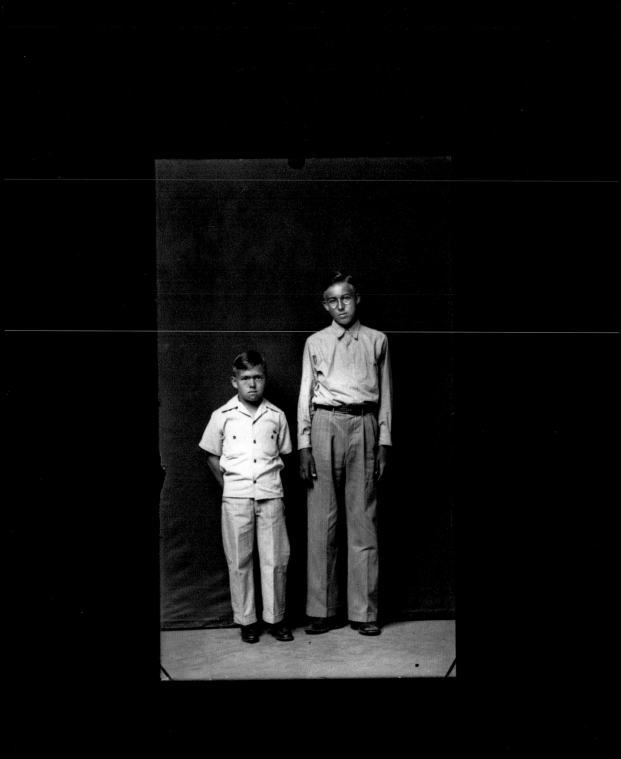

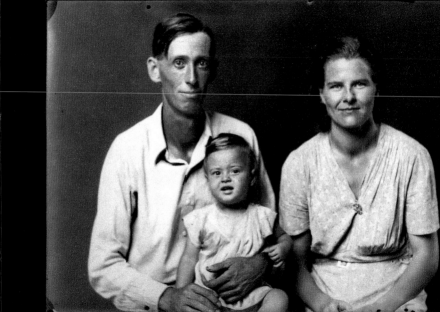

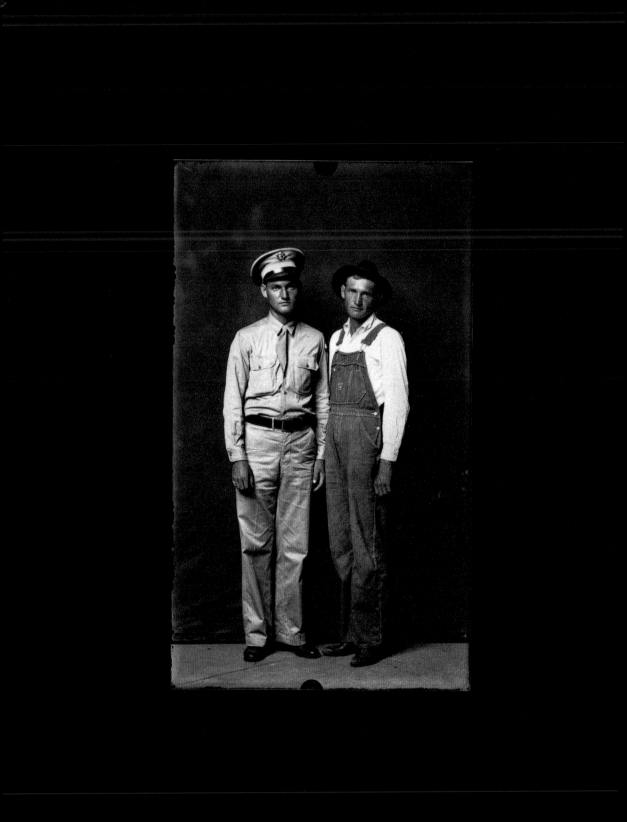

The Heber Springs Portraits

A little over twenty years ago a package of photographs arrived unsolicited on my desk at *Modern Photography* magazine. Its presence was not unusual; we routinely received hundreds of submissions each week from photographers hopeful of seeing their work published in the magazine.

When I unwrapped the package several days later, however, I found about a half-dozen portraits which were remarkable in that the subjects depicted appeared so unguarded and without pretense, so vulnerable and completely revealed.

Who was this photographer, I wondered, who had portrayed his sitters with such clarity, immediacy, and above all tenderness, and who had so absented himself from the picture that I was aware only of the person standing before the camera? A letter identified the photographs as the work of Mike Disfarmer, who had operated a portrait studio for forty years in the little town of Heber Springs, Arkansas. The letter writer was Peter Miller, a former professional photographer and the editor of the *Arkansas Sun* in Heber Springs.[1] He had come across the images, he explained, as the result of his offer to publish interesting old photos from the area.

In response, a local realtor named Joe Allbright brought Miller a group of glass-plate negatives acquired when he had purchased the entire contents of Disfarmer's studio at the time of the photographer's death in 1959. Allbright had stored the negatives in his basement, and later in his carport, for fourteen years. Perceiving their power and uniqueness, Miller not only published some of them in the *Sun*, but sent a selection of prints to me as the editor of *Modern Photography*.

I was deeply moved by the photographs and suggested to him that together we produce a book of Disfarmer's work. Miller agreed, and Allbright gener-

---

1. Peter Miller is now a trial lawyer practicing in Little Rock, Arkansas.

ously transferred the negatives to him. From the 250 or so prints that Miller then sent, I selected 66 and sequenced them in a maquette to show to potential publishers. Subsequently, I made two trips to Heber Springs to learn what I could about Disfarmer and his subjects. The resulting text (which, in slightly edited form, follows) was published along with the photographs in *Disfarmer: The Heber Springs Portraits, 1939–1946.*[2]

Critics found the photographs "an outstanding discovery"[3] and "one of the most significant bodies of work in the history of portraiture."[4] Richard Avedon included the volume in a list of twelve "indispensable" books by photographers.[5]

Over the last two decades Disfarmer's portraits have been exhibited in galleries across the United States and Europe. Yet to date he is known by relatively few images, primarily those published in the original book, which is now long out of print. The existing archive of his negatives numbers in the thousands, however. (Puzzlingly, almost all of the recovered negatives appear to date from the short time span between 1939 and 1946.)

Of the 4,200 negatives Allbright gave to Miller, approximately 3,000 were salvageable. The rest were so damaged by water and bacteria, which had destroyed the emulsion, that they had to be discarded. With the aid of a grant from the Levi Strauss Foundation, Miller spent some six months cleaning and cataloguing the remaining negatives. He then transferred the bulk of the Disfarmer collection to the Arkansas Arts Center in Little Rock, retaining approximately 300 negatives in his personal holdings. My own collection (found in a second-hand shop near Heber Springs in 1974) numbers about 400. This publication of almost 180 of Disfarmer's images, drawn from all three sources, adds significantly to the work already known.

2. Danbury, N.H.: Addison House, 1976.   3. *New York Times*, December 26, 1976.
4. *Philadelphia Photo Review*, March 1978.   5. *Bookviews*, December 1977.

The photographs are reproduced here as contact prints, that is, in the same size as the negatives. This is the format in which Disfarmer presented them to his clients. It is likely that the photographer's decision to make contact prints rather than enlargements was a purely pragmatic one. Yet it has aesthetic implications as well, since the dimensions of a photograph inevitably affect the relationship between viewer and image. The small print conveys a sense of intimacy. After all, you can easily hold it in one hand. And, like photographs in a family album, contact prints are less like monuments, more like moments remembered.

Much has changed in the photographic community since the work of the obscure portraitist from Heber Springs landed on my desk. Where there were some three or four private galleries devoted to the medium in the early 1970s, now there are several hundred. At the same time, there has developed an expanded, increasingly sophisticated audience for photographs.

Within this more complex arena, Disfarmer's straightforward document continues to touch viewers. Drawing close to these portraits, you are taken with a sense of light that derives not only from the careful technical rendering, but from the irrefutable honesty and directness of what is portrayed. To view a Disfarmer portrait is to recognize a bit of truth about the human condition. It is a recognition that, from the evidence of these two decades, has the power to override differences of geography and culture, and to transcend the passage of time.

Julia Scully
New York, December 1995

178

The Photographer

Disfarmer wasn't his real name. He was born Mike Meyer, but sometime during midlife he was taken with the idea that a tornado had carried him at birth from his natural parents and deposited him in the midst of the Meyer family, who had raised him. That there was absolutely no substantiation for this fantastic notion didn't deter Disfarmer from his conviction, which eventually led him to legally change his name.

The explanation for the unusual name selection was as strange as the obsession that caused it. "Meyer," Disfarmer reportedly told curious Heber Springs neighbors, "means 'farmer' in German." Since he was neither a Meyer nor a farmer, he explained, he would be a "dis-farmer."

Completing his bizarre identity transformation, the photographer withdrew from all contact with the Meyer family. In a small southern community such as Heber Springs, Arkansas, where social life centers around "kinfolk," this was strange behavior indeed. Yet it seemed to go relatively unquestioned by Disfarmer's neighbors.

A niece who lived in a nearby town recalled that, when she and her husband attempted to visit her uncle, he never invited them into his studio, and made it clear that they weren't welcome.[1] Understandably, they abandoned such attempts, as did the rest of the Meyer family. After years of Disfarmer's self-imposed isolation, the townspeople eventually forgot he had a large family living nearby.

1. In one of a series of interviews conducted by the author during two trips to Heber Springs in September 1974 and February 1976, and by telephone. Additional interviews were conducted by Elizabeth and Herschel Coley during March and April 1976.

By the time he had become an old man, he was a familiar figure on the streets of Heber Springs and, not surprisingly, seemed to the village children a bogeyman. They made a game of hiding near Disfarmer's studio, hoping to catch a glimpse of him. When he appeared, they ran off in mock fear.

In fact, what is most remarkable about the photographer is how little is known of him. Although he lived for forty-five years in a town of no more than 3,800 inhabitants, his life remains almost completely a mystery. It seems he confided in no one, and no one wondered why.

The few "facts" known about him have for the most part turned out to be untrue. For example, old-time residents of Heber Springs described Disfarmer as a "German." However, records show that he was born in Indiana in 1884; relatives attest that both his parents were born in America and that his father fought with the Indiana Volunteers in the Civil War. That a second-generation American was considered a foreigner in the Ozark foothills suggests part of the reason for Disfarmer's estrangement from the community.

The Meyers moved to Arkansas from Indiana in the late 1800s. They were part of a small group of families of German descent drawn by religious ties to a community called Stuttgart, which had been settled by a Lutheran minister. In this regard they were atypical of migrants to the state, who were largely from American pioneer stock. From the limited information available, it seems that Grandfather Meyer became a rice farmer and that young Disfarmer worked in the fields and later as a night watchman at a rice mill.

After his father's death in about 1914, Disfarmer and his mother moved to Heber Springs. He was thirty years old, the next to youngest of two brothers and four sisters. Disfarmer never married. He and his mother settled quietly into the community. Mrs. Meyer entered the social routine of the small town and is remembered as a fine, if a trifle "thrifty," churchgoing citizen.

At some point Disfarmer developed a serious interest in photography and set up a studio on the back porch of his mother's home. His skills were either self-taught or learned from a local photographer. In any case, his behavior did not foretell his later disassociation from his family and withdrawal from society; a niece who lived with Disfarmer and his mother during this time remembers him fondly as an affectionate and happy man.

Like other members of the Meyer family, he had a natural ear for music, playing the "fiddle" and several other instruments. This enjoyment of music, along with his passion for photography, lasted until Disfarmer's death and accounted for his only known social relationship. Albert Hendrix, a guitar-playing barber, spent musical evenings with Disfarmer inside his photography studio, playing the fast country tunes called "breakdowns" popular in that rural area. Yet, according to Hendrix, even during such relaxed and seemingly intimate occasions, the photographer "didn't say much that was personal."

A devastating tornado – of the kind that periodically sweeps across the south central states – destroyed the Meyer home, probably sometime in the 1930s. Disfarmer's mother moved in with a relative, and this may have been the impetus for Disfarmer to construct his studio on Main Street and commit himself to a career as a photographer. The building was considered very modern at the time; the studio measured about 20 by 30 feet; a big glass skylight faced north. A large camera was mounted in a partition between the studio and the darkroom; Disfarmer's small living quarters were in the rear.

He used commercially available glass plates, at first 5 by 7 inches, and in later years postcard size, 3¼ by 5½ inches. He made no enlargements; customers were presented with contact prints, for which Disfarmer charged 50 cents. (Many of these originals can still be found in the photo albums of Heber Springs families.) He continued to photograph on glass plates long after sheet film of all sizes was commonly used in portrait studios. His props were minimal: a couple of crude wooden tables and a bench, and for background a black roll-down curtain or a white wall inexplicably striped with black tape.

Disfarmer became an enthusiastic photographer, eager to record all community life, from the town baseball team to an exceptionally large haul of white bass by a local fisherman. It seemed to other residents that "his life work and his only pleasure" was photography. Regrettably, few negatives of these occasions remain; the fate of the rest is unknown.

Though Disfarmer seems to have been readily accepted as the town photographer and was often seen chatting on a Main Street corner, he hadn't a single friend in the town in which he lived and worked most of his life. (His musical companionship with Hendrix hardly amounted to friendship.) Apparently, though, he did make a minimal effort to join in the conventional social life typical of a small town, a supposition suggested by his occasional attendance at the Masonic Lodge.

On the other hand, in a community in which religion provides the social core, he was what a local resident described as "an infidel," that is, he never went to church. Moreover, Disfarmer openly admitted that he didn't believe in the Bible. This refusal to participate in even the forms and conventions of religion undoubtedly deepened the aura of strangeness sensed by all who came in contact with him. Still, though everyone interviewed agreed that he was "odd," they also acknowledged that he was "a good citizen" and a decent man who "minded his own business."

Although his oddities didn't provoke much criticism, what was referred to as his "drinking habit" did. The puritanical strain still so much a part of small-town America is evident in that this habit consisted of a "few bottles of beer" a day. Jess Barnett, former proprietor of a "beer joint" across the street from the Disfarmer studio, remembered: "Mike came down to get the paper first thing in the morning and set on the bench out there beside Haywood Grocery Store. As soon as I got open, he was ready for a bottle of beer. Mike wasn't a bad guy, he just had crazy ideas and all. He was one of those kinds that you could have a lot of fun with. No harm in him. He was just gullible enough to believe whatever you wanted him to."

The perception of Disfarmer as "harmless" was reiterated by Mrs. Ollie DeBusk: "He wasn't a good-lookin' man; he was a tall, straight man. And he was clean – his person was clean, his studio wasn't clean. [Her curious distinction is revealing.] He didn't talk very much, but we liked him because, well, he never did, as we would call it today, try to 'make' a girl. He didn't care for anything like that."

However, Bessie Utley, who assisted in the studio during some of the photographer's busiest years, may have gotten a more intimate view: "I got to where I was deathly afraid of him. You know, he was an older man. When he'd be teaching me in the darkroom how to make these pictures, I would get a little afraid, because – I don't know why. He never made any passes or anything – he was a perfect gentleman."

On the other hand, she also recollected: "He couldn't keep his hands off of me, and I told him that that's what he'd better do is keep his hands off of me. And he said he would."

Such puzzling contradictions in Utley's memory are unfortunate because, by virtue of her unique vantage point, she provided the only personal glimpses of the enigmatic personality behind the camera. "Mike Disfarmer – they can call him 'sorry' or whatever they please – but he was a fine man. I told him my story about my daughter – me wanting to put her in college – and he said that he'd let me work. Here in Depression time, you really had quite a time getting by."

According to Utley, he taught her to develop the plates, and she frequently cooked meals for him in his bachelor quarters in the studio. She added: "Mr. Disfarmer was a person that nobody would never understand if they lived to be a million years old. You know, he would make fun of the people that would come in there. He didn't exactly make fun of them, but it was like he had a brain and like we never had. . . . But, by acting like he did, it made the people kind of think he was nutty, which I knew he wasn't. They was afraid of him, yet they'd go there by the dozens. Didn't seem nobody liked Mike. . . . I think they just didn't understand him. I didn't have anything against him; he was just funny. But he wouldn't tell me nothing. Not one thing about himself. He wouldn't tell nobody."

Whatever the nature of his inner life, it was obvious to everyone that Disfarmer was proud of his profession. And for a time his business boomed, as Utley remembered: "Mike had the world by the tail, and it was a downhill pull because he didn't have no competition. They'd line up just like it was bargain basement and on Saturdays, boy, I'll tell you that was something. Them gals out in the country, they deliberately loved to have their pictures made. If they'd go to town and have their picture made one week, they were just as likely to go to town and have it made again the next. It was a fad, kind of, to go and have a hamburger and have a picture made. The only time that Mike would suffer would be when these carnivals would come through, and they'd make little photographs – real quick photographs. 'Course, they wasn't as good as Mike's."

After the end of World War II, Disfarmer's business declined. In 1959 he died, a virtual hermit, at the age of seventy-five. Carthel Haywood, owner of the grocery store across Main Street from the photographer's studio, recalled the circumstances of Disfarmer's death: "He'd gotten pretty weak. About all he'd eat was chocolate ice cream, and that's the truth. Lesby Davis came down here one morning and asked me if I'd seen Mike in the last day or two, and I said, 'no.' So [we] went over and forced the door open. And he was layin' behind the counter, on the floor. He had some newspapers under him, and he had been dead for a day or more when we found him. I don't know if he'd been sleeping on the floor all the time or not, but he was just laying out there on the floor, dead."

The People

Disfarmer probably had little expectation that his photographs would be valued after his death, except perhaps as clear records of his subjects. He left few clues to his own evaluation of his life's work, and we can only guess whether it had expressive meaning for him, and if so, what that meaning might have been.

There is no indication that Disfarmer saw himself as the maker of a historical, sociological document. Nevertheless, his work provides such a document. This raises a fundamental question: What distinguishes this product of a seemingly ordinary Main Street portrait studio from that of others on every Main Street in the United States? In seeking an answer, we must consider the character of his subjects, the time in which they were recorded, and the photographer's artistry. The character of the people portrayed is a peculiarly American character, shaped to a great degree by the rugged farm life and the small-town culture of middle America. Though that character is largely self-evident in the photographs, its specific flavor is verified in personal interviews with some of Disfarmer's subjects.

The strong family bonds apparent in these portraits were inherent in farm-centered life. The country people Disfarmer photographed were largely cotton farmers scratching bare existences from the thin soil of Cleburne County. They supplemented their cotton crops with corn, peanuts, and sorghum.

George and Ethel Gage with his mother Ida (center) and children Loretta, Ida, Ivory, Jessie and Leon

Schools would close down when whole families had to turn out to "put up" the crops. Big families, such as those Disfarmer recorded, were a practical necessity. Loy Neighbors, who was one of ten children, recollected: "We was richer than most people. There was more of us." Still, even in large families, sixteen- to eighteen-hour workdays were not uncommon, according to Mrs. Ethel Gage, the mother of seven children.

The stoicism with which hard labor and deep poverty were accepted can be read in the faces and postures of Disfarmer's subjects. For these descendants of Anglo-Saxon pioneering farmers, the struggle for existence was bitter, but it was what they expected.

One Heber Springs man described living conditions in the 1940s: "Around here people never knew there was a Depression. . . . They just didn't know that there was hard times any more than they was used to."

There seemed to be no way of breaking out of the financial deadlock in which most of the cotton and peanut farmers were caught. In the spring they would borrow money to buy fertilizer. When the cotton was sold in the fall, all of the money went to repay the loan.

After the crops were "laid by," husbands were often forced by economic necessity to leave home to find other work. Wives carried on the farming. And any available work was invariably tough physical labor. Mr. A. A. Ballantine recalled: "Shoveling gravel out of a boxcar. Right in the hot sun. You got to come 'round by sunup and leave out by sundown. You earnt your dollar. A dollar a day."

The mutual dependence and the strength resulting from surviving and enduring may be read in the demeanor of farm couples Disfarmer pictured. Ed and Mamie Barger, who were married when she was fourteen and he was twenty-six, are the subjects of one of the most moving of these portraits. Mrs. Barger reminisced about an incident in their long life together: "One

187

year, when we was planting corn, my husband took the smallpox. He had thirty-five of them blue things on the bottom of his feet and he couldn't walk. I had to go ahead with the crop. Then they broke out on me. I didn't tell him; I just tied a rag 'crost my face and I laid every bit of the corn. I was carrying one of my daughters at that time. She had scars on her face when she was born."

Even when farm families stayed healthy, the vicissitudes of the Arkansas weather provided yet another challenge. Each spring tornadoes rip through the state, and the experience of these regular disasters forms part of the collective consciousness of Heber Springs. (The fact that Disfarmer chose a tornado as the agent of his changeling fantasy suggests the pervasiveness of this experience in his environment. In fact, his life was deeply affected by the tornado that destroyed the Heber Springs home he had shared with his mother.) These fearsome phenomena unquestionably played a part in the tempering of his subjects' characters, for no matter how much the farmers toiled at forcing the land to provide a living, they were helpless before the random destruction of the twisters.

In spite of endless struggle with the ungenerous soil of northern Arkansas and recurrent catastrophes from the sky, the satisfactions of simple rural life are evident in the look and sound of these people. Their combination of pride, simplicity, and stoicism is possibly universal among those who make their living from the earth; however, the Heber Springs portraits are uniquely American. Perhaps we can find the source of this uniqueness in the social forces of the small American town. These currents still exist, for Heber Springs has changed little in the years since these pictures were made.

The Baptist religion predominates here; Protestantized, Americanized precepts of Christianity shape the public mores. Thus, a common compliment about a friend or neighbor is to note that he is "a good Christian." Another common accolade is that he "minds his own business."

Homer Eakers, Loy Neighbors, Julius Eakers, brothers-
in-law, 1945

Ed and Mamie Barger

Emma May Hoye, 1943

In Heber Springs the church is the center of social life. Nineteen churches serve the present population of 3,800. Of these, seven are Baptist, one Catholic, the rest various Protestant denominations. And religion is not limited to Sunday morning; churches hold Wednesday-night prayer meetings as well. During the 1940s the weekly *Cleburne County Times* reported the names of those who had "made the decision" to join Christ during revival meetings the previous week. Circuit-riding preachers still served needy souls scattered in the almost roadless back country around Heber Springs as late as 1945.

The force of evangelical belief is at least partially responsible for the fact that Cleburne County has been dry since 1944. Before its prohibition referendum was approved, Heber Springs was a rip-roaring frontier town. On a Saturday, according to Mrs. Ollie DeBusk: "You couldn't get down to Main Street for people on the street fightin'. And on Saturday mornings, we would wake up and wonder who was killed last night."

Prohibition apparently brought peace to Main Street. With cynical humor, former saloon keeper Barnett suggested the impact of organized religion in the little town: "The good people voted me into the chicken business in 1944. Brother Smith, a Methodist; Brother Palmer, a Baptist; and Deacon Bob Woods, they were instrumental in getting a petition for people to vote on it. And I built three small birdhouses and dedicated each to them: the 'Smithsonian Institute,' the 'Palmer House,' and the 'Wood Memorial Building.' And I invited them – every one – up to get a free chicken and they all accepted. They'll do that, good people. They'll take whatever you can give them."

Provincial, inbred, descended from generations of Anglo-Saxon farming stock, longtime residents suspected outsiders of any sort. The 1930 federal census reported the ethnography of Cleburne County as follows: 5,802 native white males; 5,557 native white females; 8 foreign-born white males; 3 foreign-born white females; 3 Negro females (temporary servants to tourist, no residents).

In 1976 there is still not one Black person to be seen on the streets of Heber Springs, and a handful of families account for a large segment of the community.[2] According to a minister who had a parish in Heber Springs during the 1940s, clannishness and suspicion amounted at times to an economic boycott of outsiders: "I remember seeing farms between here and Little Rock where an outsider would come in with money and [he would] paint, build fences, buy machinery, and in about three or four years, they'd just sweat him out, and the place was sold. They had a way of just ostracizing the outsider."

Eighty-three-year-old Judge Neill Reed added a footnote to the accounts of insularity: "A fellow moving into Arkansas had to be here a hundred years before he would be anything except a foreigner. My daddy came here from upstate New York. He bought the first newspaper the town ever had, he established an abstract company, [he] served in many official positions, he was Grand Master of the Oddfellows in 1912. He reared a family here, done more for this county than any man in the history of the county. Until his death, some people [still] called him a 'damn Yankee.'"

2. Current statistics suggest that the character of Heber Springs and Cleburne County has changed little in the twenty years since this essay was written. The town's population has grown by only 2,000 and the number of churches by eleven, and the breakdown of denominations is proportionally the same. Cleburne is still dry, and according to the 1990 census there are but six African Americans among its citizenry of almost 20,000.

The Time

Disfarmer gave visual expression to this closed, homogeneous society – one that had at its core hard work, fundamental Protestantism, and family ties. His picture of this society, conveyed through a cross section of its members, acquires a compelling force because of the time in which it was made.

The emotionally charged national spirit of hometown rural America during World War II pervades the Disfarmer portraits. Men to whom bib overalls had been a daily uniform stand self-consciously in military garb; women wear lapel insignia indicating the military units of husbands or sons; children appear patriotically in uniform. Describing the circumstances of one such image, Mrs. Mattie Bishop said of her son Lecil: "This little one thought he could be a soldier, too, and he sent that picture to his older brother in [the] service."

Not as obvious, yet crucial to understanding the emotional fabric of the Heber Springs portraits, are other ways the war colored almost every one of them. The Killion brothers, for example, went to Disfarmer's studio the day Clifford left for the service; Walter and Thelma Pettus had their portrait made with his family and by themselves during the week they were married, while he was on leave; the Navy cap and middy blouse worn by Emma Mae Hoye were chosen to please her husband, who was in the Navy and to whom she sent the portrait.

The anguish of families whose men were in combat is also a part of the Heber Springs portraits. It is written in their faces, yet frequently understated in verbal recollections. Twin sisters Eula Hines and Euda Hinesley also sent their portrait to their husbands, both of whom were fighting in Germany. Said Eula Hines: "Of course, they didn't have any place to carry it;

they was in action all the time. After we sent it out there, they sent it back. They said they couldn't keep anything like that."

While she was pregnant with their second child, nineteen-year-old Bonnie Dell Gardner had her photograph taken to send to her husband overseas. The nine Bullard sisters and their mother went to town in a horse-drawn wagon to have a family record made for their brothers overseas. (The only other times Nancy Bullard Donaldson remembered the entire family going somewhere together were "for a funeral of a very close family member or friend.") Byrum Bullard kept the photograph in his shaving bag throughout the war.

Because at the time she was so distraught about her son, who had been wounded, Mamie Barger cannot remember having her picture made with her husband to send to the boy. She did recall: "They [the government] sent me a card that I could come to New York and visit my son in seventy-two hours, but I didn't have no way of gettin' there. We didn't have no money saved up."

Like thousands of Americans, many men from Heber Springs served for the entire four years of the American involvement in the war; some of them spent much of this time in combat zones. Many were killed; some endured years as prisoners of war. Most of these men had never ventured outside Cleburne County before being drafted. The experience of war remained a never-assimilated nightmare in their quiet, insular lives. Celebrations marked the homecomings, and sometimes they too were occasions for visits to Disfarmer's studio. Such were the circumstances when Loy Neighbors and his two brothers-in-law stood for a portrait. According to Neighbors, he had just returned from Germany, where he had been a prisoner of war. On the way home he had bought a suitcase full of whiskey with his back pay: "And my brothers-in-law was helpin' me drink it. I'd been gone so long,

Festus and Violet Pettus with Walter Pettus and wife Thelma (backrow), Wendell, Marion and Joann (front row) 1945

Walter and Thelma Pettus, 1945

I wasn't homesick or anything. I had a wife and a couple of children and I'd forgot their names. When I got back to the United States, you know, I thought I was all right wherever I was; I was home, right then."

Thus, in his studio on Main Street, Disfarmer caught a microcosm of small-town America at a point when its endurance was being severely tested. The way that test was met is portrayed in the faces of his subjects.

The Photographs

The power of the Heber Springs portraits, then, lies both in the character of the people and in the time in which that character was revealed. Yet neither element is unique; that character could doubtlessly have been duplicated in a cross section of a thousand small towns across the nation during these same years. It is in the clarity of the revelation that the essential strength of this collection lies.

Disfarmer was just a small-town portraitist, yet he avoided the portrait studio artifice, popular elsewhere, which turned each subject into a mask of smiling sameness. He developed a strong personal style perhaps best characterized by its artlessness. North light gave an even overall illumination by which he recorded every detail of his subjects' appearance as they stood for the relatively long exposures required by the slow-acting emulsion on the glass plates. Disfarmer did a minimum of arranging and posing of his subjects (the rough stools and benches his only props) and obviously never tried to coax a smile or gesture from them. He pressed the shutter when his presence was least intrusive.

Perhaps it was Disfarmer's perception of his own alienation from his environment that permitted him the artistic distance needed to record these plain country people so clearly. With directness and simplicity, he achieved a revelation of character that more sophisticated photographers have attempted with greater technique but perhaps no greater success.

In their power and intent, Disfarmer's portraits are comparable to the work of three widely known and appreciated photographers. In considering how these accomplished artists strove for techniques that would reveal essential human character, we can better appreciate what Disfarmer achieved with elegant, if naive, simplicity.

For many years famed studio photographer Irving Penn made portraits using north light and presenting his subjects (both exotic and ordinary) in a straightforward style against plain backgrounds. His series of small-tradesmen, done in this style, appears to have been an effort to capture the essential qualities of each trade by eliminating all formal differences in the portraits other than the subjects themselves. Though his approach is reminiscent of Disfarmer's, his virtuosity, including an exquisite sense of composition and (in some of his work) color, produced pictures that ennoble the sitters. In contrast, Disfarmer's people are life-size and believable. The viewer confronts them as equals.

The power of such direct confrontation was recognized by Diane Arbus. She stared straight at her subjects and they stared back. Arbus made portraits of force and clarity, as did Disfarmer; however, she chose subjects who were strange or unconventional – nudists, transvestites, the mentally retarded – and accented their strangeness with the harsh glare of direct flash. Even when her subjects seem normal, Arbus's work is disturbing.

Perhaps closer to Disfarmer in spirit, though concerned with a much broader human landscape, was the German portraitist August Sander. He set himself the task of portraying no less a subject than the German people over a span of twenty years, between the two world wars. His is probably one

Mary Stone Bullard (front, center) with daughters: Nancy, Stella, Blanche, Gladys (front row);
Sarah, Ida, Betty, Elsie and Lela (back row), 1943

of the most remarkable photographic oeuvres ever produced, each portrait a superb document delineating the individual personality of the subject. But each also captures those characteristics that mark the sitter's class, profession, and even attitudes.

Sander's stage was a grand one compared to Disfarmer's. And certainly he had a much larger vision – that of showing the faces of an entire society and, through them, suggesting the social and political forces of a particular time and place. Compared to Sander's, Disfarmer's milieu was limited, yet he succeeded in presenting this small stratum of society as symbolic of a larger one. Within their given ends, each managed to produce work of simultaneously specific and general meaning.

Disfarmer's Heber Springs portraits obviously function on several levels. On the surface, they present a clear and honest record of what people looked like in that part of America at that specific time. Beyond this statement is another, which has to do with the quality of life and the spirit and sentiment of Americans undergoing a traumatic episode. Through accidents of time and place, Disfarmer had as his subject a microcosm of rural America at an emotional and historical turning point.

Depression-era America was magnificently recorded by the Farm Security Administration (FSA) photographers. Their work has been, and continues to be, widely published and exhibited. But visual documentation of the period between 1941 and 1946 is scanty.

The best images of the 1940s are of the war experience. Photographers of that era – W. Eugene Smith, Robert Capa, and Margaret Bourke-White, for example – went with their cameras to where American troops were fighting. At the same time, home-front photography largely reinforced a propaganda campaign that showed the supportive efforts of the civilian population. Until now little photography has come to light which would fill the gap between the FSA record of the 1930s and the extensive domestic photojournalism of the 1950s.

Disfarmer's record of some of the citizens of one small town in the south central United States is a step in filling that void. From what we know and can surmise, the self-contained and remote society of Heber Springs was severely shaken, creating an atmosphere that gives these portraits their special historical character. Ultimately, what underlies the effectiveness of the work and what moves us is Disfarmer's genius in allowing his subjects' souls to show. In this sense, the photographer and the people of Heber Springs collaborated in an artistic venture more profound than either could possibly have imagined.